G000067013

THE STORY OF ABRAHAM

WORKS BY
Edward Leigh Pell

==================

THE PELL BIBLE STORIES
ILLUSTRATED

Book 1
The Story of Abraham -- As Told By Isaac

Book 2
The Story of David – The Idol of The People

Book 3
The Story of Jesus – For Little People

Book 4
The Story of John – The Beloved Disciple

Book 5
The Story of Joseph – The Dreamer

Book 6
The Story of Paul – As Told By Himself

THE STORY OF ABRAHAM

AS TOLD BY ISAAC

By
EDWARD LEIGH PELL
Author of "Secrets of Sunday School Teaching"

ILLUSTRATED

South Oxford Press
Oxford, New York

Originally published by
Fleming H. Revell Company
1920

Book 1

ISBN-13: 978-0615983462
ISBN-10: 0615983464

2014 Editor: Robert G. Yorks

South Oxford Press
2139 County Road 3
Oxford, New York 13830
Web site: www.southoxfordpress.com
Email: southoxfordpress@live.com

CONTENTS

I

FATHER AND SON

An OLD man, tall, and straight as an arrow, with a great wealth of grayish white hair falling in curls about his shoulders, a flowing beard white as the snows of Lebanon covering his brow, wonderful eyes that looked out upon you from beneath great white crags, -eyes as deep as the wells he used to dig in Gerar -wells with stars shining in them -stars that twinkled, -eyes that sometimes flashed like his Damascus blade and sometimes melted with tenderness like the eyes of a gazelle –such was my father as he appeared to me when I stood before him a little child three score and ten years ago.

Yet though to my childish eyes he looked more like an angel of God than a man, I never knew the time when I was afraid of him, for he was as lowly in heart as he was princely in bearing. When a stranger came to his tent he never permitted a servant to stand before him, but always insisted upon serving him with his own hands, and when he sat beneath the great oak and I sat in his lap it was as if two children were playing together –only now and then when telling me a story he would suddenly become as one inspired and begin to speak in a strangely solemn way, and presently a great storm would rise in his bosom and his eyes would flash like the fire of the clouds and his voice would peal like thunder among the mountains.

Many and wonderful were the stories which my father told me in those beautiful days of my childhood. There were stories about God; stories about giants; stories about the wonderful city from which my father came. And sometimes there were stories which those who knew not the God of heaven love to tell about their own gods. For my father did not keep me in ignorance of the ways of the heathen lest I should unwittingly fall into their snares. One day when he had told me the story of the creation as it had been handed down in our family from our father Noah, he said:

"Now listen while I tell you the story as I used to hear it from one of my father's heathen servants when I was a boy. Once, a long, long time ago, when as yet there was no heaven and no earth, when Apsu (the primeval Ocean) and Tiamat (Chaos) mingled their waters, when no land was formed, when no reed was seen, when as yet nothing had been called into being, when no name was named, when no fate was fixed, then the gods were created. First Lahmu

Lahamu came forth. Then after ages had passed Anshar and Kishar were called into being. Long were the days, then came forth other gods. Then Apsu and Tiamat rebelled against the rule of the new gods and Tiamat brought forth a brood of monsters to war against them. The news was carried to the chief of the gods who commanded his followers to go forth against Tiamat and the monsters, but they were afraid and refused to obey. At length Marduk went forth endowed with great power and invincible weapons. He carried a lightning flash charged with blazing fire and a net containing a great hurricane. He met Tiamat in combat, cast the net over the monster, let loose the hurricane and drove the wind down her throat to burst her body. He ripped her up with his sickle-shaped sword and cut her skin into two parts and with one part he made the vault of heaven. Then he established the earth and the underworld. Next he made the stars for a habitation of the gods. He set up the Zodiac; ordained the year and divided it into months, appointing three stars to each month, and then he set the moon in the heavens to rule the night and to fix times and seasons. Afterwards he made the beasts of the field and creeping things and last of all he made man."

I was very young when my father told me this strange story, but I remember how very absurd it seemed to me and how I pitied the poor heathen, and how glad I was that our God was not like their terrible gods. And I remember how glad I was the next day when he told me a far more beautiful story which made me think better of the heathen, though I am sorry to say it did not give me a better opinion of their gods. This is the story as he told it to me:

"Once the great gods within Shurippak took secret counsel to bring a flood upon the earth. There was Anu, their father, and there was Bel, the warrior, Ninib, their messenger, and Innugi, who directed them, and there was also Ea, the god of wisdom. Ea had a friend among men whom he desired to save from the flood and so he appeared to him in a dream and told him what the gods intended to do. And he said unto him: 'Thou man of Shurippak, build thee a ship and forsake thy possessions and take heed for thy life and bring unto the ship living seed of every kind. And the man whose name was Sitnapistim built a great ship six stories high and one hundred and eighty feet in breadth and covered it within and without with pitch. When it was finished he brought into it all his possessions —his silver and gold and goods and cattle —besides beasts of the field and living

12

creatures of every sort. Then one evening the ruler of darkness sent a great rain and Sitnapistim took his family into the ship and shut the door and gave the guidance of the ship into the hands of Puzur-Bel, the mariner. At dawn a great black cloud came up and Rimmon thundered in the midst thereof, and before it went Nebo and Marduk, even as messengers went they over mountain and plain; and Uragal tore up the anchor and Ninib went forth and the storm followed after. The Annunaki lifted aloft their torches and lighted all the land with their brightness. The whirlwind of Rimmon reached unto heaven and day was turned into night so that no man could behold his fellow. Then the gods became frightened and drew back into the heaven of Anu; they crouched like hounds and sat cowering. And Ishtar cried as a woman in anguish and bewailed aloud over the destruction of the people, who now filled the sea like the spawn of fishes. And with her wept the gods; they were bowed down, their tears flowed, their lips were pressed together. For six days and six nights the tempest blew and the flood covered the earth, but on the seventh day the storm and the deluge which had fought like a great host, was abated, the sea sank to rest and the hurricane was spent. Then Sitnapistim looked out upon the waters and called aloud, but the race of man was turned again to earth and their habitations had become a swamp. He opened the window and the light of day fell upon his face and he bowed down and wept, for lo! all was sea. After twelve days the dry land appeared. To the land of Nisir the ship floated and the mountain of Nisir held it fast. For six days the ship rested and on the seventh Sitnapistim opened the window and sent forth a dove. And the dove flew this way and that, but she found no resting place and she returned. Then he sent forth a swallow. And the swallow flew this way and that, but she found no resting place and she returned. Then he sent forth a raven and it left; it ate, it waded, it croaked, it did not return, for the waters were abated. Then Sitnapistim went forth out of the ship and offered up sacrifice and poured out a drink offering upon the mountain top, and the gods smelled the sweet savor and like flies they gathered round the sacrifice. And Ishtar, the lady of the gods drew near and said, 'Never shall I forget these days. Now let the gods come unto this offering; but let not Bel come for he sent the flood and gave my people to destruction. But when Bel saw the ship then was he wroth and filled with anger because a man had escaped destruction, and he demanded to know who had revealed his purpose to Sitnapistim. Then Ninib opened his mouth and spake: 'Who but Ea could do this thing since Ea knoweth all things?' Then spake Ea and said unto Bel: 'Ill-advised wast thou, O counsellor of the gods, that thou didst send the flood. On the sinner lay his sin and on the transgressor his transgression, but let not all the innocent as well as the guilty be destroyed. Let the lion and the leopard, let famine and pestilence slay mankind but let there be no flood again. I divulged not the counsel of the gods to Sitnapistim in words but in a dream did he learn it.' Then went Bel into the ship and took Sitnapistim by the hand and led him forth: and he blessed him and his wife and he said: 'Now let Sitnapistim and his wife be as we who are gods and let them dwell afar off at the mouth of the rivers.' And the gods led them away and gave them a dwelling place even at the mouth of the rivers."

When my father told me this story I expressed in my childish way my astonishment that there should be anybody in the world so ignorant as to believe such things, and he replied:

"Why, my son, that is the story as they tell it in the land of learning, even in the sacred city of Ur, the city of schools and libraries and of wise men learned in all the wisdom of the world. But" –he added- "one day you will understand that men may be very wise in the things that pertain to the world and yet very foolish in the things that pertain to God: for it is given to man to search and find out many mysteries of earth and sea and sky, but no man by searching can find out the mysteries of God. We can only know of God what he chooses to reveal to us concerning himself, and if we turn away from him and forget what he has revealed to us and then try to imagine what he is like and how he acts, we shall only imagine foolish things —as foolish as the story I have told you."

"But," I asked, "do all the wise people of Ur believe such stories?"

"No," he replied, "for in Ur as elsewhere there are a few sincere souls who cannot be satisfied with heathen vanities but in their hearts they long for God, even as the wild doe when pursued by the hunter panteth after the water brooks. Once I heard a man praying to the Moon-god. His heart was full of anguish and he was trying hard to reach the ear of his Creator, and this was his prayer:

" 'Lord, long-suffering and full of forgiveness, whose hand upholds the life of all mankind! In heaven, who is supreme? Thou alone, thou art supreme. In earth, who is supreme? Thou alone, thou art supreme! O Lord, my sins are many, my transgressions are great. I sought for help and none took my hand. I wept and none stood at my side. I cried aloud and there was none that heard me. To my God, the merciful one, I turn myself, I utter my prayer. O My God, seven times seven are my transgressions: forgive my sins!'"

I can never forget how my heart went out in tenderness toward the poor heathen as I listened to this prayer, for I had often heard my father pray to Almighty God in almost those very words.

My father was learned in all the wisdom of the Babylonians and it was his desire that I should have all the educational advantages which he had enjoyed, but he was unwilling that I should be exposed to the evil influences of the heathen schools and he therefore undertook to teach me himself after the manner of the ancients. And so every day I went and sat down by his side and took heed to the words of his lips. First he would tell me a story of the past. Then he would give me a proverb to learn by heart, and then he would tell me another story, after which he would talk to me about God. As I grew older he told me more and more about the wonders of the world, and at length he turned my eyes toward the heavens and taught me the mysteries of the stars. Then he turned my eyes back to earth again and spread before me the wonders of the land from which he came. One day —it was a joyful day! —he pictured to me the glories of the sacred city of Ur. He told me of its beautiful streets; of its glorious temples and how they were built, story upon story; of the magnificent libraries and how the books in them were written; of the beautiful ships that sailed from its harbor and the strange countries to which they went and the wonderful treasures which they brought back.

While he was speaking, my eyes wandered toward the old family tent and then to the cluster of smaller tents occupied by my father's followers standing near, and when he was through I said:

"I wish I was there. Why did you leave all those beautiful things and come over there into this lonely land to live in a poor old tent?"

"Ah, my son," said my father with a strangely solemn look in his eyes, "that which is unsavory cannot be eaten without salt, neither is there any taste in the white of an egg."

II

A WONDERFUL VISION

THE next day when I took my place at my father's side he held up before me a beautiful apple. He had cut it open but had carefully put the two halves together again.

"Look at this, my son," he said, and as he spoke he let the pieces fall apart in his hand.

"Ugh!" I exclaimed in disgust; for the worm had done its deadly work and the apple was as foul within as it was fair without.

He was silent for a moment, then casting the pieces aside he said:

"You asked me yesterday why I left Ur. When I was a child the city of my fathers fascinated me, for it was fair to look upon and I saw only the outward appearance; but when I became old enough to look within I turned from it with loathing, for sin like a worm had eaten its way through its heart and it was full of death and all uncleanness. The people of Ur adorned their bodies with beautiful robes and their speech with beautiful words, and their homes with beautiful vases and rugs, and their streets with beautiful temples and statues and libraries, but their

19

secret thoughts were full of darkness and their lives were unspeakably vile."

And then he went on to explain how it happened that the people of his country became so terribly wicked.

"When God made men," he said, "he did not leave him to himself but visited and communed with him until man came to know God even as a son knows his own father. But when sin came into the world men turned away from God and shut him out of their thoughts, and not having the fear of God before them they went on deeper and deeper into sin. By and by trouble came upon them and sorrow and they felt that they must have a God; and as they had forgotten the God of heaven they undertook to make gods of their own; and their thoughts being evil they made for themselves gods that were evil, and having such gods before them they gradually grew worse and worse until every imagination of the thoughts of their hearts was only evil continually."

"But did everybody forget God?" I asked.

"No, my son," he replied. "Here and there in the world God had his sincere worshippers who handed down his name to their children and their children's children, but they were few and far apart as fountains in a desert, and when I was a child I think our family was the only one in all Ur that served the God of heaven.

And then he told me how his mother had talked to him about these things when he was a little child and how sad she was when she spoke of them and how his little heart had been set on fire with desire to do something to keep the name of God from disappearing from the earth.

"My mother," he said, "was a devoted worshipper of the God of heaven and so was my brother Haran, but she died when I was young, and by and by Haran died also, and after that it seemed to me that I was alone in the world; for though my father believed in our God, his heart seemed to be set upon the ways of the heathen and he often went to their temples, and my brother Nahor went with him.

"My people were farmers and cattle raisers and like many others of the same calling we lived in the city and went forth every morning to our fields and pastures. Sometimes I would go to the farm and take a flock of sheep far out on the plain and spend the day watching over them while they grazed. Usually there was little to do and I would sit for hours with my eyes fixed upon my sheep while my thoughts would wander away to distant pastures. Often I thought of God and of the beautiful world he had

21

made for us and of the ingratitude of his creatures who, having received all things at his hands, had turned away to worship gods of their own making. And often as I thought of these things I wept and cried aloud unto my God. One day while I was pouring out my soul unto God there came to me a wonderful vision."

Here my father paused and a strange far-away look came into his eyes. I waited a moment and then begged him to go on but he did not notice me. At length he said:

"I cannot tell you of that vision, only you must know that the God of heaven appeared to me and told me that he had set me apart to preserve his name in the earth, and that I must leave my country and kindred and go to a distant land in the West which he would show me, where I could separate my family from all heathen influences and train them up to keep the way of the Lord. Moreover he promised me his blessing and declared that in my seed all the nations of the earth should be blessed."

Then he went on to tell me that when the vision was gone he lay still upon his face as one dead, but presently a strange warmth filled his heart and an unutterable joy thrilled through his whole being. He sprang to his feet and hurried his sheep back to the fold and then hastened to his father and told him of the wonderful commission which God had given him and urged him to leave Ur and go to the land to which God had called him. His father scanned his face anxiously for a moment and then the tears came into his eyes and he said:

"Truly it is from the Lord, my son, and I cannot say anything against it."

But just then Nahor came in and when my father repeated his story his brother laughed in his face and begged his father to pay no attention to his foolish dreams.

"I turned away," said my father, "with a heavy heart for I knew I could not overcome the strange influence which my brother had over him and that night I wept bitterly upon my bed and asked God to show me what I should do. It did not occur to me to leave home without my father, for as you may know, among my people it is not considered meet that a son should leave his parents so long as they remain upon earth to bless him. The next day I met a friend who had just returned from the West and I found him full of enthusiasm over that wonderful country. It was almost as rich, he said, as the richest grain lands around Ur, and what was better the land was thinly settled and there was abundant room for all. This I knew would appeal to my brother, for we had many flocks and herds and it was daily becoming more and more difficult to find grazing lands for them. And so I persuaded my friend to go home with me and tell my brother all that he had seen.

"The next morning I found that Nahor had caught my friend's enthusiasm and when I went to my father he readily consented to my plan. Then I hurried to my friends and tried to persuade them to go with me, for I knew that it was impossible to make the journey unless we could get together a caravan of sufficient size to secure ourselves against attacks from lawless hordes of the desert. At first I talked to them about the commission which God had given me and tried to interest them in my great purpose, but they only winked at each other and smiled and tapped their foreheads and passed on. Later I talked to them about the wonderful opportunities of the great west and I was more successful. Indeed I had so little difficulty in persuading them that our company was soon made up and at the next full moon we turned our faces from Ur and our great caravan began to wind its way up the river road toward Haran.

Abraham and his family starting out for the land of Cannan

"It was a long journey and very exhausting to my father who was now old and feeble, and when we reached Haran he insisted that he could go no farther. And so we pitched our tents under the shadow of the city walls and scattered our flocks and herds on every side as far as the eye could reach. The country was so rich and our flocks and herds increased so rapidly that many of our friends decided to settle permanently in the land, but I was anxious to get away from Haran, for it was almost as full of heathen abominations as Ur, and besides my heart was set on the great commission which God had given me. And so when my father died and the days of mourning were passed, I gathered my possessions all together and having received directions in a vision of the night I set my face steadfastly toward the land of the southwest. None of my people went with me except my wife and Lot, my brother Haran's son, but I had many followers and servants, and my caravan was so large that the people of the land through which we passed stood in great awe of us. We stopped for some days at Damascus where we traded and then renewed our journey toward the river of Canaan. One beautiful morning in the early spring we crossed the river a few miles below the great lake and made our way slowly up the steep ascent beyond. When we reached the top of the ridge a scene of wonderful beauty burst upon our vision. Within a great wall of blue mountains stretched around the horizon lay a vast green sea of hills and valleys bathed in the mellow light of the morning sun. A hundred hillsides were dotted over with beautiful flowers –red and white and pink and golden and purple. The sky was melodious with the songs of birds and great golden butterflies flitted lazily about in the warm sunlight.

" 'As beautiful as the garden of the Lord!' " I exclaimed as I stood with Lot drinking in the scene.

" 'True; and where can we hope to find a fairer land to dwell,' cried Lot with enthusiasm. 'See it is but thinly settled: I can count but four flocks in all the land. Why not build a city on yonder hill and gather our people around us and bring our wanderings to an end."

"But I said to him:

" 'My son, it was not for this that I left my country and my kindred. God has called me out from among my people to build up his name in the earth and not to build up cities where heathen abominations may abound.'

"The young man turned from me with a sigh, for he had never become reconciled to our wandering life and his heart yearned for the city even as the parched grass yearns for the morning dew.

"We turned toward the south and at sunset we pitched our tents in a beautiful plain where our flocks would find abundant pasture. That night God appeared to me in a vision and told me that I had at last reached the land which he had set apart for me, and assured me that the whole country should one day be occupied by my descendants. He did not give the land to me, for he did not want me to be permanently settled again lest my heart should become entangled in the things of the earth and I should lose sight of the great commission which he had given me. And so ever since that day I have been a stranger and a sojourner in the land, wandering hither and thither as God directed me, trusting him for all things, keeping my heart ever detached from the things which the heathen seek after and ever looking forward to the great day when the knowledge of God shall cover the earth and when in my seed all the nations of the earth shall be blessed.

"And this, my son," said my father, putting his arm around me tenderly, "is the reason why I prefer this simple tent above all the glories of the city of my childhood. If I can here raise my son to keep the way of the Lord and shun all heathen enchantments I shall think it a small matter that I gave up my country and became a wanderer and a sojourner in a strange land!"

As he spoke these last words he looked toward the setting sun and its glory filled his face. But in his eyes I was sure I saw another light —a light like that which shines in the eyes that have opened upon the glory of God.

III

STRANGE HAPPENINGS IN A STRANGE LAND

THE morning after his vision my father arose very early and calling six of his servants sent them to gather great stones from the hillsides. As they brought them to him he laid them one upon another in the form of a hollow square until the walls were nearly as high as a man's loins. Then he had them fill up the hollow place with earth and smooth it over, and while the wood was being placed in order upon it one of the servants was sent to bring a lamb from the flock and another went to call the people to the sacrifice. Meanwhile my father hastened to his tent and when all was ready he came forth clothed in a long white garment, and taking his place by the altar solemnly offered up the lamb as a burnt offering unto God. Then as the smoke of the sacrifice ascended and while the people stood looking on in silent awe he lifted up his hands to heaven and blessed the name of the Most High God; after which he turned and blessed the people and dismissed them to their daily tasks.

Thus did my father begin to magnify the name of the God of heaven in Canaan and from that day the smoke of the morning sacrifice has not ceased to ascend to our God in the sight of the heathen.

By and by the grass gave out in the pastures and my father plucked up his tent-pegs and removed to a plain not very far from the city of Salem, and there again he erected an altar and called upon the name of the Lord. And thus he went on from place to place, ever going toward the South and everywhere building an altar unto God until at length a chain of altars ran like fortresses throughout the land. Not long after reaching the South Country the rainy season failed and the grass began to parch like leaves in an oven, and my father was compelled to drive his flocks and herds to Egypt for sustenance; but so soon as the drought was over he returned to Canaan and after remaining in the South Country for a short time started on another slow journey through the land.

My father's flocks and the flocks he had given his nephew Lot had now grown so large that it was no small matter to find pasture for them. As a consequence there was much strife between his shepherds and Lot's and this went on from bad to worse until my father saw that there was danger of a serious breach between the two families. One day he called Lot aside and had a frank talk with him about the matter.

"We are brethren," he said kindly but firmly, "and this strife must cease. Our flocks and herds are too large to dwell together any longer and it is better that we should separate. Now, my son, go out and look over the country and let me know what part of the land you wish for yourself. I want you to have your choice. If you go to the right hand I will go to the left, and if you choose the left hand I will go to the right."

That was always my father's way. Under the promise of God the whole land belonged to him for his descendants, yet in the kindness of his heart he not only offered to divide with his nephew, but insisted that he should have the first choice. Never was there a more magnanimous soul.

That evening as the sun was setting Lot climbed to the top of the highest hill in the neighborhood and carefully examined the face of the country. Presently his eyes fell upon the great plain that is watered by the river which runs into the Salt Sea. It is beautiful country of great fame for its fertility, and in those days was dotted over at its lower end with beautiful cities, like the white ships that dotted the green sea beyond the harbor of Ur. It was a tempting sight –too tempting for one of Lot's disposition to resist – and after gazing until the gathering twilight shut out the beautiful vision he hastened down the hill to my father's tent.

"I will choose the country of the plains," he said abruptly.

"Very well," said my father quietly, "and may mercy and peace be with you."

My father said nothing more, for he was cut to the heart. Not that he cared on account of the land, for he would not have turned toward the cities of the plain under any circumstances, but he could not be insensible to his nephew's selfishness and want of gratitude, and it hurt him deeply to find that the young man's heart still yearned toward heathen cities, for he had heard that the wickedness of Sodom exceeded even the abominations of Ur.

The next day Lot set his face toward the East and within a month he had pitched his tent under the shadow of the walls of Sodom, and the next time my father heard from him he had given up his pastoral life and gone to dwell in the heart of the city. Yet I would not have you think that he was actually led astray be heathen enticements, for I have heard that he never gave up the worship of Almighty God and that he often rebuked the people of Sodom for their sins.

Nevertheless the man paid dearly for his choice. He had hardly settled in Sodom before the vassal kings of the plain threw off the yoke of their eastern conqueror and lord, Chedorlaomer, and the next year the great king swept down upon them with a mighty army and punished them terribly for their rash conduct.

"One morning," said my father, from whom I learned the story, "I was sitting in the door of my tent near the little city of Arbah, when I heard a distant shout, and lifting up my eyes I saw a man running swiftly toward me. As he came nearer I saw that his garments were rent and his head was covered with dust, and I knew that he was a bearer of evil tidings.

" 'News! My lord, news!' he shouted as he bounded into my presence and threw himself on his face before me.

" 'Alas! My lord,' he cried excitedly, 'the great king of the East came down upon Sodom with a mighty army and has laid waste and carried all the people away; and your kinsman Lot they have carried away also.'

"My heart fainted within me but I quickly revived, and springing to my feet called aloud for my steward. I sent him with a message to my confederates –three Canaanite chiefs with whom I had an agreement for our mutual protection –urging them to come to me at once with all the men they could bring. Then I sent out servants over the country with orders to all my people to drive in their flocks and herds in haste and report at my tent. In a little while they began to arrive and as rapidly as they came I set them to work. The women baked bread and parched wheat that we might have food to refresh ourselves by the day, while the men put new strings in their bows and polished such spears as we had and made new ones by cutting long wooden stakes and sharpening them at the end and hardening the point in fire. Then two-score swords which I had bought at Damascus were brought out to be polished, but when we uncovered them they smote upon our eyes like the noonday sun.

"At last all was in readiness and a little before sunset I had three hundred and eighteen armed men drawn up before my tent door awaiting our confederates who presently came with three hundred more. We greeted them with a mighty shout and then we started off together at a great pace in pursuit of the enemy, who I had learned was now on the way toward Damascus with a great burden of prisoners and spoil. We marched all night without stopping and when the sun was up we lay down in a wood and rested until the cool of evening and then we started again. Thus we went on night after night until at last one morning an hour before dawn we came upon the enemy's camp fifty miles southwest of Damascus. I divided my forces and just as the day began to dawn we pounced upon the camp from opposite sides with a shout that froze the hearts of the waking hosts with terror. They sprang to their feet with frightful cries and for a moment rushed blindly about utterly beside themselves; then by a common impulse, like a great herd of frightened kine, they tore off toward the desert, leaving all their spoil and prisoners behind them. I left a score of our men in charge of the camp and sprang after them, and all that day we pursued them and ceased not to smite them until the sun went down.

"When we returned to the camp Lot came to meet me and threw his arms about my neck and kissed me, and we wept together. Then he told me that I had rescued all the people that had been carried away with him; not one of them was missing. It was a joyful hour and I felt that God had richly rewarded me for all my trouble.

"We were many days on our way back to Arbah, for our men were greatly burdened with spoil; but the tidings of our victory flew like eagles before us and all along the way the people came out in great crowds

to greet us. At last came the king of Sodom, leading
the remnant of his army that had escaped, and when
they saw us they lifted up their voices with a mighty
shout in our honor. The king's heart was melting with
gratitude and he overwhelmed me with kindness and
finally insisted on escorting me on my way. When we
reached the valley of Shaveh we found the king of
Salem waiting to greet us. As we approached he
came forward to meet me in the name of the Most
High God. At the sound of that name my heart
bounded within me for I had never been told that the
king was a worshipper and priest of the God of
heaven, and I sought to honor the name of my God
by offering him as the priest of the Most High a tithe
of all the spoil which God had given unto my hands.
The king had brought out great baskets of bread and
skins of wine and for an hour my weary soldiers lay
upon the grass and ate and drank and told the story of
their adventures to the people that crowded around
them. At length as evening wore on, the king of
Sodom came to me and said:

" 'I must now leave you. Give me my people, but
keep the goods for yourself.'

" 'No, my lord,' I replied, 'for I have lifted up my
hand in a solemn promise to my God that I would not
take anything for myself or my people even to a

thread lest it should be said that the king of Sodom had made me rich. I only ask that these men of Canaan who went with me shall have what they have taken.'

"He urged me but I would not be persuaded and then he wished me peace and went his way. And Lot, whom I had fondly hoped would take warning from his fearful experience, turned from me and followed the king."

IV

HEAVENLY VISITORS

W<small>HEN</small> my father reached home he found a great multitude waiting to do him honor, but his strength had now utterly forsaken him and as soon as he had saluted the people he retired to his tent. As he dropped upon his bed his soul fainted away and for a long time my mother leaned anxiously over him lest the spark of life should pass from him. By and by he revived, but that night a horror of great darkness fell upon him and he grew weary of his life and requested of God that he might be gathered unto his fathers.

"What is my end?" he cried, "that I should prolong my days? All these years have I waited and now I am old and still I have no child to inherit the promise of God, and Lot whom I had thought to make mine heir has forsaken me and all this fearful struggle to rescue him has been for naught and I have no reward. Moreover, I have brought down upon my head the enmity of a powerful king and before him I and my people shall vanish as dry leaves before a devouring fire, and no man shall rise to shield me."

"Abraham?" said a voice in the dark. "Fear not, Abraham, and be not discouraged, for I am thy shield and thy exceeding great reward."

But the anguish of his spirit was great and he could only cry out:

"What can you do for me, Lord, seeing that I am now old and childless and there is no one to be my heir except my steward – this Eliezer of Damascus."

"Eliezer shall not be thine heir, Abraham, " said the voice firmly; "thou shalt have a child of thine own who shall be thine heir. Rise and come forth."

And my father sat up and the streams of life began to flow afresh through his soul and he grew strong and arose and went forth and stood without the tent door. And the voice said:

"Look up and behold the stars and see if thou canst count them."

And my father looked up. It was a clear moonless night and the heavens were ablaze with stars, like the gems upon a king's crown, and my father, who was learned in the wisdom of the heavens, knew that no man could number them. As he stood with upturned face his eyes wandered from one constellation to another until he was overwhelmed with a sense of the majesty and power of Him who had brought them into being and who was even now speaking to him.

And he threw himself upon the earth and lay very still before God. Then came the voice again:

"Abraham, as these stars which thou seest so shall thy seed be."

And my father believed the word that was spoken to him and his peace came again to his bosom and he arose and went back to his bed and slept.

And yet month after month and year after year passed by and the promised child came not.

One day while my father was sitting in his tent door in the heat of the day he looked up and saw three strangers coming up the road. He hastened out to the roadside to intercept them, for it was always his delight to show the hospitality of God to strangers, and when they came up he saluted them and said:

"My lords, I pray you turn aside and rest awhile and I will fetch water to wash your feet and a bit of bread to comfort your hearts and when you are refreshed you shall go on your way."

They thanked him and came and sat beneath the tree near the tent door while my father hastened to serve them. He brought water for their feet and then hurried into the tent and told my mother to make some bread as quickly as she could; then he ran to the herd and selected a calf tender and good and gave it to a young man to kill and dress it. Finally when all was ready he set the veal and bread with butter and milk before his guests and as they ate he stood by them beneath the tree and talked with them. He soon discovered that two of his guests behaved toward the third with great deference and were loath to speak in his presence, and he began to wonder if heaven had not at last bestowed upon him that rare privilege which our people have ever craved –the privilege of entertaining the angels of God. Presently the stranger who seemed to be of higher rank than the others asked abruptly:

"Where is Sarah thy wife?"

My father was startled by the question, not only because the Stranger was acquainted with my mother's name but because it is not considered meet among our people for a man to inquire of the woman of one's family; but he answered quietly that she was in her apartment and waited to know what would come of the matter. The Stranger was silent for a moment and when he spoke again my father was more astonished than ever, for his voice was now strangely like the Voice he had heard in the vision of the night.

"Truly," he said, "I will return to thee according to the time of life and thy wife shall have a son."

My mother who was in the tent near by heard his words and could not help laughing within herself at the thought.

"Why did Sarah laugh?" asked the Stranger quickly, "Is any thing too hard for God?"

"I didn't laugh," called out my mother, who was now greatly frightened.

"But thou didst laugh," said the Stranger firmly.

Then they arose to go and my father went with them to see them on their way. As they reached the top of the hill they looked toward Sodom and the Stranger, who my father now realized stood in some mysterious sense for the God of heaven himself, turned toward the other two and said:

"Shall I hide from Abraham that which I am about to do, seeing that I have bestowed great honor upon him and will make of his descendants a great and mighty nation, and all the nations of the earth shall be blessed in him? For I know that he will command his children and household after him and teach them to keep the way of the Lord so that the promise of God to him may be fulfilled."

Then he turned to my father and said:

"I have heard evil reports of Sodom and Gomorrah and I am going down to see if the people have done altogether according to the reports that have come to me."

He turned to go on his way with the others, but my father suddenly planted himself in front of him. It was the boldest deed a mortal man ever did, but the thought of the peril that threatened Lot, whom my father still loved, had made him desperate.

"Will you destroy the righteous with the wicked," he cried? "Suppose there are fifty righteous men in Sodom —will you not spare the place for their sakes? Far be it from thee to slay the righteous with the wicked. Shall not the Judge of all the earth do right?"

"If I find fifty righteous persons in Sodom," replied the Stranger, "I will gladly spare it for their sakes."

He spoke so graciously that my father was encouraged to venture further and he said:

"Now that I who am but dust and ashes have ventured to speak to the Lord, let me go further; suppose you should lack five of the fifty —will you destroy the city for the lack of five?"

"No," he said, "If I find forty and five righteous persons there I will not destroy it."

But my father was now full of fear lest there should not be so many and he said:

"Suppose there are only forty there?"

And he answered:

"I will not destroy it if I find forty righteous persons there."

My father hesitated a moment and then he said:

"Let not my Lord be angry and I will speak again. Perhaps there will not be but thirty there?"

"I will not destroy it if there are thirty there," said the Stranger quietly.

But my father's heart was still overwhelmed with fear and he could not let the matter rest.

"What if there are only twenty," he asked.

And He answered, still quietly, still patiently:

"I will not destroy it if there are twenty there."

My father was now trembling from head to foot lest he should go too far, but the vision of Lot's face soon steadied him and he determined to make one more venture.

"Oh, let not the Lord be angry," he cried, "and I will speak but this once. Suppose there are only ten found there?"

And the answer came as quietly and patiently as before:

"I will not destroy it if ten are found there."

My father stood aside and bowed low and the Stranger went on his way, and after watching him until he was out of sight he turned and slowly retraced his steps. That night his heart was heavy with foreboding and his sleep fled from him and as he tossed restlessly upon his bed he cried again and again:

"If I had only asked him to save the city for one!"

At last toward dawn he fell asleep, but as the sun arose he was suddenly awakened by a violent trembling of the earth. He lay still for a moment wondering what it meant and presently it began again. He could feel the earth reel to and fro like a drunken man. He grew faint and sick and could hardly raise his head, but at last he summoned up all his strength and sprang up and hastened out of his tent and up the road in the direction of Sodom. When he reached the top of the hill he threw up his hands and uttered a cry of horror. For the whole country of Sodom and Gomorrah was enveloped in a smoke as black as midnight, and through the smoke shot here and there great streams of light as of liquid fire which pierced the heavens and fell back a fiery rain upon the earth.

The fire of God had licked up the cities of the plain!

That evening a messenger from Zoar came to Arbah bringing the awful news. At sunrise, he said, there was a fearful quaking of the earth and the people of Zoar saw a great shaft of smoke and fire shoot up from the midst of Sodom, and presently there came down upon all the plain showers of flaming bitumen, and the whole country was as it were cast into a great furnace and consumed. Not a soul in all Sodom and Gomorrah, said the man, had escaped to tell the news. For a long time my father supposed that Lot was dead, but one day a man from Zoar who stopped to rest at his tent told him that Lot and his two daughters had come to the village on the morning of the calamity, having been warned by angels to escape, but that they were so terrified that they would not stay, but fled to the mountains near by. His wife, said the man, had started with them, but lingered behind and was overtaken by the fiery shower.

V

A PROMISE FULFILLED

It was in the following spring that the promised son was born and the dream of my father's life was fulfilled. My mother told me that when I was carried to my father for his blessing the great deeps of his mighty heart broke up and he wept for joy. Then he hurried out of the tent and called his people together and offered a great sacrifice unto the Lord. On the eighth day when I was named he gave a great feast in my honor and many of his friends came to rejoice with him because the Lord had given him a son in his old age, and again when I was weaned he gave a greater feast to which he invited a great multitude from all the country round about.

But the days of my father's rejoicing passed swiftly by and soon a great shadow fell upon his heart. Away back in those trying days when my father and mother were waiting for the fulfillment of the promise my mother gave up all hope of having a son of her own and gave my father her maid, Hagar, to be his secondary wife, according to the custom of our people, thinking that it was perhaps in this way that God intended that his promise should be fulfilled. By and by Hagar had a son and she was very happy in the thought that he would be my father's heir. But she was doomed to a terrible disappointment and when I came she could not conceal her bitterness toward me and naturally in the course of time her son Ishmael began to share her feeling. The boy mocked me even from my infancy and so provoked my mother that at last she told my father she could stand it no longer and insisted that he should send the woman and her child away. It nearly broke my father's heart and for three days and nights he could neither eat nor sleep. At last one night God visited him in a dream and told him not to be troubled about the child and his mother but to do as my mother had said, and assured him that he would take care of him and would make a nation of the child's descendants because he was my father's son.

It seemed a terrible thing to do and my father wept bitterly over it, but it was his way when God told him to do anything to do it whatever the cost, and the next morning he hugged the child to his bosom and sent him away with his mother. He gave Hagar a bag of money and told her that he would set apart a goodly portion for her son and that he would provide for her all her days, and then he gave her a basket of bread and a skin of water and she went away. Years afterwards we learned that the poor woman in her grief lost her way in the wilderness and that her bread and water gave out and she and her son came near perishing by the way. They wandered until they were too weak to go farther and then she laid the child beneath a shrub and went off a little distance from him; for, as she said she could not bear to see him die. And she sat down and wept bitterly and cried out in her anguish unto God. Presently she heard a voice from heaven:

"Hagar," said the voice: "What aileth thee, Hagar? Be not afraid, be not discouraged, for God hath heard the voice of the child. Go and take the lad in your arms for I will make of him a great nation."

She sprang up with a low cry of joy and ran to her boy and strained him to her bosom. Then looking about her she spied a fountain which somehow she had not seen before, and she ran to it and filled her waterskin and brought it to her boy and lifted him up and he drank and his spirit revived. And God led them to Paran where they soon found a home.

From the time that I was weaned I was my father's constant companion. My mother often said –with a pardonable trace of maternal jealousy in her voice- that I had no need of a nurse for I was never out of my father's lap, and I hardly think she intended it for an exaggeration for I cannot recall that he was ever willing for me to get out of his sight. People called me my father's shadow, but I was more; I was his very substance. His heart fed on me. Moreover my love for him was even as his love for me; my very life was bound up in a bundle with his life. And time, which so often digs a great gulf between father and son, only deepened our devotion. I never grew ashamed of his tenderness toward me. Even when I was six feet tall he never offered the morning sacrifice that I did not go and stand by his side just as I did when a little child that he might lay his hand upon my head when he prayed. Thus we journeyed along the way together and the peace of God was upon us, and as time went on my father's cup of joy again filled up to the brim.

One night my father lay awake upon his bed thinking of the Promise and of the wonderful way in which God had worked out all things toward its fulfillment, and as he thought upon it his heart melted with gratitude. Suddenly a vague sense of foreboding mingled with awe came upon him. He lay still wondering what it meant and presently he came conscious of someone standing near him. Then out of the darkness came a voice, gentle and low.

"Abraham?"

"Here am I," he answered.

"Take now thy son," said the Voice with a strange tenderness, "thine only son, Isaac, whom thou lovest, and go to the land of Moriah, and there offer him as a burnt offering upon one of the mountains of which I shall tell thee."

My father made no reply for the sword had pierced his soul and he lay still upon his bed as one dead. After a time he began to revive but the awful words again flashed through his mind and he pressed his lips tightly together to smother the cry of anguish that broke from his heart. He raised his hands toward heaven beseechingly and then pressed them together tightly upon his bosom that seemed about to burst.

"Is it possible!" he cried to himself –but no sound escaped his lips- "Is it possible! Is this the end of all my hopes? O my son, my son, my son!"

He fainted away and when he revived again he strove desperately to master himself.

"Be still my soul!" he said sharply: "Should I who have received good from my God –should I not be willing to receive evil also? When he gave I blessed him, should I not bless him when he —when he-"

But a vision of his son's face passed before him and the sword again pierced his soul. Presently he revived again.

"What?" he cried. "Do not my heathen neighbors offer their children to their gods? And shall a servant of the Most High God fall behind them? If they are willing to sacrifice their sons to such gods as they worship shall I refuse my son to the God of heaven? Shall I ---"

But again the vision of the lad's face came before him and his spirit fainted away.

He lay still for a moment and then suddenly sprang up in his bed.

"I *will* obey him!" he cried. "It will kill me to do it but I will obey him. And I will trust him. I don't know what he means but he will keep his word. He *must* keep his word. If I slay my son he can give him back to me again. He *will* give him back to me for he will keep his word."

He fell back upon his bed exhausted, and presently a strange peace came over him and he dropped into a gently slumber.

VI

THE BRAVEST THING A FATHER EVER DID

HE AWOKE at dawn and as he lifted his heart toward God the awful vision of the night before flashed through his mind and again his soul fainted away. But he quickly revived and remembering his own word of promise he calmly prayed for strength and then arose quietly and left the tent. He called two of his servants and gave them orders to prepare for a journey; and then he called me.

"My son," he said calmly, but without looking into my face, "I am going to the land of Moriah to offer a burnt-offering unto Almighty God and I want you to go with me."

I could not understand why he should go so far to offer a sacrifice, though I knew that he had a deep reverence for sacred places, but he offered no explanation and I said nothing. We started off at sunrise. My father rode on an ass, for he was too feeble to walk, and I walked by his side, and behind us followed two servants, one carrying an armful of dry wood for the altar and the other bearing in one hand a fire-carrier full of live coals and in the other a small bag of charcoal to keep the fire alive. We went on our way all that day and all the next in silence for I could not persuade my father to talk. He was very pale and his lips were pressed tightly together and his face was set as a flint toward Moriah; he would not look either to the right or the left. At last on the third morning we came to the foot of a mountain and my father descended from his beast and took the fire-carrier and a knife which one of the servants carried in his girdle, and telling the servants to tarry until we should return, he motioned to me to go with him, and together we started up the mountain. As we went on our way I said to him:

"Father?"

"What is it, my son?" he replied, gently.

"We have the wood and the fire, but where is the lamb for the burnt offering?"

He stopped suddenly and his whole frame quivered, but he quickly started forward again and presently he said with a strange calmness:

"My son, God will provide a lamb for the burnt-offering."

At that instant a horrible thought flashed through my mind and I grew faint and dizzy and reeled like a drunken man. What? Was I –was it possible- did he intend to offer *me* for a burnt-offering? Me?

I had often heard how the heathen nations offered their sons to the gods and I knew that one of our neighbors had carried his first born on a journey to a heathen temple and returned without him, but the possibility that such a fate would ever overtake me never occurred to me until that moment. For a time I stumbled blindly along my way –though I strove hard to walk erect lest my father should see my agony, and as I went the fear deepened to a settled conviction that my father had seen a vision and that God had required his son at his hands. For a time a wild storm raged in my mind and I had a fearful struggle with myself, but at last the tempest began to subside and I found myself saying to my soul:

"Shall a son dishonor his father? Should not a son be as his father? If my father can thus yield himself unto the will of his God shall I not yield myself unto the will of my father who has always stood to me in the place of God?"

I wondered afterwards that I could not have thought so calmly but I suppose the God of my father must have laid his soothing hand upon me. A merciful numbness now came over me and I walked on with my father without concern for what was before me. At last we came to the top of the mountain and at once set about gathering stones for the altar. We arranged the stones in a hollow square and then I made my father rest while I filled up the hollow square with earth and placed the wood in order upon it. Then as I stood back my father arose and drawing a thong from the folds of his robe advanced toward me. His face was ghastly white and great drops of cold sweat stood out upon his brow.

"My son," he began, but I saw that his lips were quivering and I said quickly:

"Never mind, father, I understand; it's all right."

I put my arms about his neck and kissed him as quietly as I could and then I turned and stretched myself out upon the altar and closed my eyes. I was still strangely calm for the soothing hand of my God was still upon me.

I could feel my father's cold, damp, trembling hands as he tied my wrists with the thong and bound me to the altar. Presently I could feel his breath upon my cheek and I knew that he was leaning over me and gazing into my face. My heart went out to him with a pity that made me forget myself and I silently prayed unto God for him. Then I felt his quick kiss upon my lips and I knew that he had straighten-ed himself up and raised his knife for the deed. The next instant a strange voice fell quick and sharp upon my ears.

"Abraham! Abraham!"

I opened my eyes and my father stood beside me, his right hand raised on high still grasping his knife, his ghastly face turned toward heaven.

"Abraham," cried the voice again, "lay not thine hand upon the lad, for now I know that thou fearest God seeing thou hast not withheld thy son, thine only son from me."

My father dropped the knife upon the ground and lifting both hands to heaven cried out:

"My God! My God!"

He could say nothing more, for the great deeps of his long pent-up heart now broke wildly forth and he threw himself upon me and wept aloud. Then he raised himself and looked into my eyes with an unutterable joy and then impulsively covered my face with his kissed. At length he became quiet and raised his head he spied a ram caught by his horns in a thicket. He picked up his knife, quickly cut the thong that bound me and lifted me up and then we hastened together to the thicket for the ram which God had indeed provided for the burnt-offering. I stood by my father as he offered the ram upon the altar and when he prayed he laid his hand upon my head. Never have I heard my father pray as he prayed that day.

When he had ended, the voice again came from heaven:

"Abraham," said the voice, "because thou hast obeyed me in this thing and hast not withheld thy son, thine only son from me, truly in blessing I will bless thee and in multiplying I will multiply thee, and thy descendants shall be as the stars of heaven and as the sand that is by the seashore, and in thy seed shall all the nations of the earth be blessed."

As we came down the mountain my father's face shone like the face of an angel of God and all the world about me was as fair as the garden of the Lord. The glory of God was upon the grass and trees and flowers; the birds sang with a sweetness I had never known before, and the morning air refreshed my soul like the blood of grapes. When we came to our servants my father spoke to them with a gaiety that startled them, and as we went on our way homeward he talked incessantly, as one whose heart is overflowing with a secret joy. My father never told my mother of his experience nor did he ever mention it to me until a few days before he died, when he told me the story of his vision and his awful struggle. Nor did I speak of it until the day after his death when I told the story to my twin sons that they might realize the greatness of their grand-father's spirit and that they might understand that while the God of heaven requires implicit obedience he abhors human sacrifices; for he is not like the gods of the heathen who would have us do violence to the natural affections which he has placed in our hearts; for the gods of the heathen feel not, but our God is a God of compassion.

REBEKAH AT THE WELL

VII

THE BEAUTIFUL REBEKAH

M Y MOTHER was now very old and feeble and we could see that she was slowly passing away, like a brook in the drought of summer. My father watched over her with tender solicitude, for they had walked together for a hundred years, but she was weary and longed to go, and at last one evening in the late autumn as the sun was setting, she gave us both a tender farewell and turned away in peace to her long rest.

The next morning at dawn my father went to Arbah and sat in the gate of the city and when the people were gathered together he arose and addressed them. He told them of my mother's death and then he said:

"As you know I am a stranger and a sojourner in the land and I have no possession among you and I have come to seek a burying place that I may bury my dead out of sight."

When he had ended one of the elders of the city stepped forward and bowing low to my father said to him:

"Hear us, my lord. You are a mighty prince among us; in the choice of our sepulchers bury your dead; for there is no man among us who would withhold his sepulchers from you."

My father, in the princely manner which had not forsaken him in his old age, bowed very graciously, first to the elders and then to the people standing near and said:

"If it is indeed in your hearts that I should have a place to bury my dead among you I beg you to entreat for me to Ephron, the son of Zohar, that he may let me have the field in which is the cave of Macpelah for as much money as it is worth."

Just at that moment Ephron came up and when he was told what my father wanted he came forward and said with great courtesy:

"Nay, my lord, I would not have you pay me for the field; it is yours; here in the presence of all my people I give it to you; take it and bury your dead."

At this my father bowed very low again and said:

"But if you will give me your field I must give you money for it; accept it I pray you and I will bury my dead."

"My lord," said Ephron, "the land is worth four hundred shekels of silver, but what is that between us? Take the land and bury your dead."

The price named was several times greater than the value of the land, but my father without a word opened his bag and weighed out the silver to him in the presence of the people, and thus the field of Ephron in which was the cave of Macpelah was made over to my father for a possession.

That was always my father's way; though humble in spirit as a little child, yet in all his dealing with men he behaved as a prince of God.

After my mother's death my father clung to me more closely, if possible, than ever before, yet his devotion, even now that he was old enough to be childish, was never blind nor selfish, for he was always ready to deny himself for my happiness. I could see that he was now thinking of another great sacrifice which the will of God was about to require of him and that he was daily trying to strengthen himself for it. If the promise of God was to be fulfilled he must stand aside even in his old age and allow another to come and take his place and occupy the larger place in his son's affections. One day he called his steward and said to him:

"I am now old and know not the day of my death. Put your hand beneath my thigh and take a solemn oath that you will not take a wife for my son from among the daughters of Canaan, but that you will go to my father's country and take a wife for him from among my own kindred."

"But suppose she would not be willing to come to this land," said the steward; "shall I take your son thither?"

"No! never!" said my father earnestly; "whatever you do beware that you take not my son thither. The God of heaven who took me from my father's home and led me to this land and promised to give me this land for my children, he will send his angel before you to direct you and you shall take a wife for my son from my kindred"

And the man took a solemn oath that he would obey my father in the matter.

"If the woman will not come with you," said my father, "you shall be clear of your oath, but under no circumstances must you take my son away from this land."

My father made great preparations for his important mission and when the steward started the next morning for Haran he had a great train of servants and camels bearing costly gifts for my wife and her parents. The steward was a most faithful servant of my father and a devout worshipper of my Father's God, and in his devotion to his master's interests he often turned for direction to the God of heaven.

When he reached Haran it was in the cool of the evening, near the time when the maidens of the city were accustomed to come out to the well near the gate for water. He caused his camels to kneel down by the well and while they were resting he lifted up his eyes toward heaven and prayed.

"O God of my master, Abraham," he said, "I pray thee send me good speed this day and show kindness to my master Abraham. Here I stand by the well and presently the maidens of the city will come out to draw water. When I say to a maiden, "Let down that pitcher that I may have a drink of water, if she should say, 'Drink and I will give your camels drink also, 'let her, I pray thee, be the maiden whom thou hast provided for my master's son, and thereby shall I know that thou hast shown kindness to my master."

He had hardly finished his prayer before a maiden came to the well with a pitcher upon her shoulder. The steward gazed intently upon her as she hastened down the steps to fill her pitcher. When she came back her eyes were shining like the stars of heaven and her cheeks were as red as the blood of grapes and he thought she was as beautiful as my mother the first day he laid eyes upon her. Bowing low he said to her:

"I pray you, let me drink a little water out of your pitcher."

And the girl with a rare maidenly grace let down the pitcher upon her hand and said sweetly:

"Drink my lord," –and presently she added- "and I will draw water for your camels also."

When he had drunk she emptied the pitcher in the trough and hurried down the steps and brought up another, then another, until the camels had finished drinking. Meanwhile the steward stood silently pondering the matter. Presently he said to himself:

"I cannot be mistaken; surely God has answered my prayer."

He took from beneath his robe a little bag and opened it and as she turned to go he said to her:

"Whose daughter are you?" and added: "Is there room in your father's home that we may lodge?"

"I am the daughter of Bethuel the son of Nahor," she answered modestly. "Yes, my lord, we have plenty of room that you may lodge with my father."

The steward lifted up his eyes to heaven and devoutly gave thanks to God; then while the maiden looked on in wonder he took out of his little bag a beautiful nose-ring and a pair of costly bracelets and handed them to her. She was so astonished that she could not speak but took the jewels and ran home as fast as she could.

"And where is the man?" asked her brother Laban excitedly when she had told her strange story. And he hurried out to the well. In a little while he returned with the steward and his servants and his father received them with great hospitality. After the steward had washed his feet and rested they set food before him and urged him to eat, but he said:

"No, I cannot eat until I have told you my errand.'

He was a man of business and he was so faithful that he never allowed himself to think of his own comfort while any duty remained to be attended to. And so he told them that he was the steward of Abraham the brother of Nahor, and that God had greatly blessed his master and that he had become very great and was very rich in flocks and herds and camels and servants; that his master's wife had borne him a son in his old age and that his master had sent him to take a wife from among his own kindred for his son. And then he told them of the plan he had adopted at the well to find out whom God had appointed to be the wife of his master's son.

"And now," he said, when he had told his story, "if you will deal kindly and truly with my master tell me, and if not let me know at once so that I may know what to do."

The girl's father and brother arose and went into the women's apartment and after a little while they returned and the father said:

"This matter is evidently from the Lord and we cannot say anything against it. Rebekah is before you. Take her and let her be your master's own wife even as God has spoken."

At this the steward bowed his head and gave thanks to God, and then he went out and opened up the goods he had brought and presently the servants came in one after another bearing great burdens of precious things –jewels of silver, jewels of gold, costly robes and rugs and vases; and the steward presented them to Rebekah and to her mother.. It was a wonderful display such as they had never seen before and they could not conceal their delight at the great blessing that had thus suddenly come upon them. Then the steward sat down and they ate and were very merry.

The next morning the steward arose early and asked permission to leave at once that he might return without delay to his master. Rebekah's mother and brother now began to entreat that she should be allowed to remain a few days longer but he begged them not to hinder him seeing that God had prospered him in his journey.

"Well then," said the mother, "we will call Rebekah and see if she is ready to go."

And they called her. When she came her father said to her:

"Will you go with this man?"

"I will," she replied.

And so the steward took her and her nurse and turned his face toward Canaan.

In those days we were living in the South Country and the journey was long and weary and it seemed to me that the steward would never return. Every evening at sunset I would put on my festival robe and walk out in the fields and look up the road toward Arbah to see if the camels were coming. One evening as I walked to and fro wrapt in meditation I looked up suddenly and saw the steward and his train coming along the plain hardly three furlongs away. As I looked I saw a woman alight from her camel and cover her face with her veil and I knew that she was my wife. My heart now throbbed fast within me. Presently the steward hurried his camel on ahead and as he came up he saluted me and told me that God had greatly prospered him and in a low voice he said:

"And she is as beautiful as your mother was when her fame was throughout all the land.

At last they came up and I went and took my wife by the hand and led her to the tent that had been occupied by my mother, and there at the tent door my father greeted her and lifting his hands to heaven pronounced upon her the most beautiful blessing I ever heard. And thus the lovely Rebekah became my wife, and my heart melted with tenderness toward her, and I was comforted after my mother's death.

VIII

SUNSET

MY FATHER spent his declining years in great peace. The storms of life had all passed and left him in his place like a mellow apple hanging alone upon the tree in the quiet golden days of autumn. Unlike other old men he spent his days not in dreaming of the past but in sweet anticipation of the future. His faith in God had become an impregnable fortress and he could stand upon its walls and look out into the future and see the fulfillment of God's promise as a landscape spread out before his eyes. For twenty years I was childless, but he never suffered a moment's anxiety; he could still look forward and see my children playing about my knees. He would sit in his tent door at sunset and as the golden light flooded his thoughtful face that far-away look would come into his eyes and he would see as in a distant picture the whole land of Canaan covered with his descendants, worshippers of Almighty God, and he could see a great stream of blessing flowing out of the land into all the world and carrying joy to all the nations of the earth, even as a river flowing out into the desert causes the grass and flowers and trees to grow upon its banks.

When my twin sons, Esau and Jacob were born my father was very happy and desired to depart, since he had seen his last desire fulfilled, but he was spared to us for fifteen years longer and my two boys were brought up on his knees. I can see him now as he used to sit beneath the great oak near the tent door with his arms around my sons –an old, old man with a long snowy beard and kindly eyes peeping out from beneath great shaggy white brows, and close against his beard on either side a little round face with rosy cheeks, one fair, with auburn hair and eyes as blue as the sky, and the other dark, with eyes and hair as black as the raven's wing. Those were joyful days to my boys for my father told them many beautiful stories just as he had told me when I was a child; yet their joy was tempered with awe because of his great age, for they seemed to feel that their grandfather was an ancient prince of God who must have been present at the creation of the world.

We were living in the South Country in those days but when my father saw that his time was drawing near he begged me to go back to the plains of Mamre near Arbah so that he might be sure of a final resting place by the side of my mother. And so one day I plucked up my tent-pegs and we returned to the old home place where my mother died. And there I watched over my father as the cords of life gradually loosened to the end. One day he called me and my two sons to his side and gave us his final blessing. Soon afterwards his mind wandered back to the past and the tears came into his eyes, and he turned to me and said:

"I should like to see Ishmael before I go."

And I sent a servant in haste to Shur to tell Ishmael that our father's time was at hand and that he desired to see him. On the third day Ishmael came. I went out to meet him with dread but when I looked into his face I saw that my message had awakened only the tenderness of the past without its bitterness, and I put my arms about his neck and kissed him and we wept together. I brought him into my father's tent and there the great rough man of the desert became a child again and threw himself upon my father's face and wept aloud. My father's spirit fainted away, but presently he revived and summoning up all the strength that remained to him he lifted his hands to heaven and pronounced a beautiful blessing upon my brother. He fell back exhausted upon his pillow and when he again opened his eyes I saw in them that far-away look which I had so often seen when he was looking upon the vision of God. At last he closed them and a moment later he passed away as quietly as a little child falls into his evening slumber.

We buried our father in the Cave of Macpelah by my mother's side. The sun was setting as I came forth from the cave and its golden light fell upon my two boys who stood waiting for me. I put my arms around them and three weeping children made their way home in the gathering twilight.

THE END